Chasing the Cod

JERSEYMEN IN CANADA

WRITTEN BY DOUG FORD

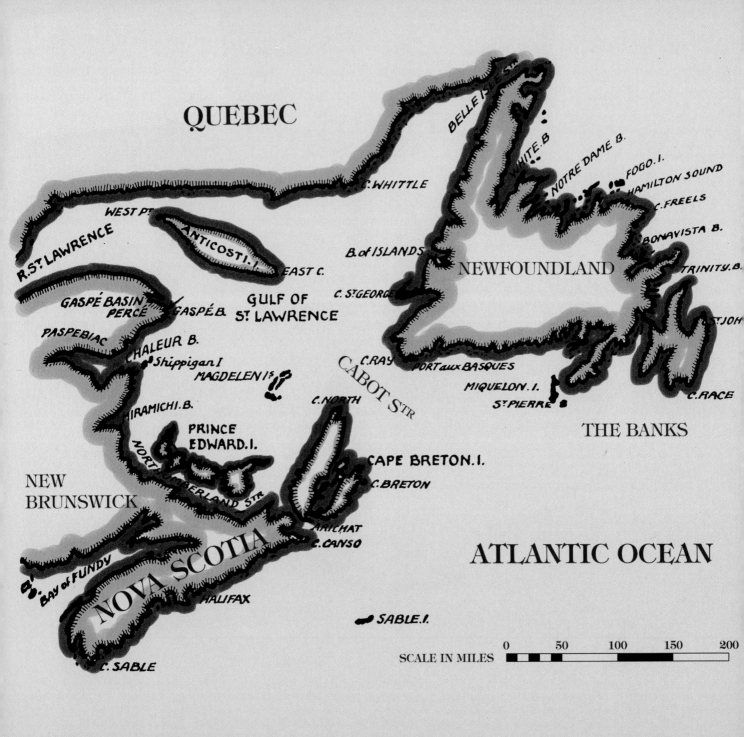

QUEBEC

C. WHITTLE

BELLE ISLE STR

WHITE. B

NOTRE DAME B.

FOGO. I.

HAMILTON SOUND

C. FREELS

BONAVISTA B.

TRINITY. B.

WEST Pt

ANTICOSTI. I.

B. of ISLANDS

NEWFOUNDLAND

R. St. LAWRENCE

EAST C.

C. St. GEORGE

St. JOH

GASPÉ BASIN
PERCÉ

GASPÉ B.

GULF OF
St. LAWRENCE

PASPEBIAC

CHALEUR B.

C. RAY

PORT aux BASQUES

Shippigan I

MAGDELEN I^s

CABOT STr

MIQUELON. I.

C. RACE

MIRAMICHI. B.

C. NORTH

St. PIERRE

PRINCE
EDWARD. I.

THE BANKS

NEW
BRUNSWICK

NORTHUMBERLAND STr

CAPE BRETON. I.

C. BRETON

ARICHAT

C. CANSO

ATLANTIC OCEAN

NOVA SCOTIA

Bay of Fundy

HALIFAX

SABLE. I.

C. SABLE

0   50   100   150   200

SCALE IN MILES

A Belle Anse fishing barge c.1895

Over 500 years ago the Jersey fishermen were sailing over 3,000 miles over the Atlantic Ocean to take part in what became known as "the fisheries". Their quarry was the Atlantic cod – *gadus morhua* - that moved into the shallower waters around the Newfoundland Banks and the Gulf of St Lawrence.

Although seasonal in origin, over the centuries, these first contacts led to long-term contact and settlement in what was to become known as Canada. The Island merchants who equipped these expeditions developed into the "Jersey firms" who were to play a major role in the economic development of their island home – but at the expense of the Canadian regions, especially the Gaspé peninsula of Quebec.

At a different level, the fisheries offered some islanders the opportunity for advancement and this meant moving to Canada on contract or permanently. These became *les Jerriais au Canada* - the Jerseymen in Canada - and this is the story of the community in Point St Peter.

Chasing the Cod

JERSEYMEN IN CANADA

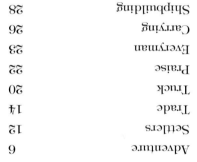

"It is a memory now, it is just a memory and people who are aged will talk about it …but the Canadian adventure of Jerseymen is now a memory"

Before leaving Jersey in the spring the fishermen all attended church in St Brelade as this would be the last time they could take communion until they returned in late September/October - this custom, "Le Communion des Terre-neuviers", began in 1611.

The Canadian Adventure

According to tradition Channel Islanders along with their Breton and Norman neighbours were fishing off the Grand Banks as early as the fifteenth century well before the Cabots claimed Newfoundland for King Henry VII in 1497. Channel Island activity in this new found land is recorded in the many place names as well as local records. In 1582 Pierre de la Rocque referred to Jerseymen voyaging to Newfoundland in his will in which he left his sons equal shares in the ship "which is now unloading after she voyaged to Newfoundland" and in 1591 Jean Guilleaume was fined 300 crowns in the Royal Court for selling his Newfoundland cod to the French in St Malo instead of bringing it back to Jersey. While he was governor (1600-1603) Sir Walter Raleigh promoted the Newfoundland trade and Jerseymen were amongst the first permanent settlers in Newfoundland at Harbor Grace.

From Newfoundland it is only natural that fishermen would have followed the shoals of cod and it is entirely possible that, again with their Breton and Norman counterparts, they were active in the Gulf of St Lawrence by 1504. When the Frenchman, Jacques Cartier, "discovered" Canada in 1534 amongst his 61 men were six with island surnames - Guilleaume de Guernezé, Anthoine, Fleury, Ollivier, Le Breton and Colas and when he described Bradore Bay on the Labrador coast he wrote *"... there great fishing is done"*.

Once caught, the cod had to be preserved before it was taken back to market over 3,000 miles away in Europe. Two methods were used for preserving the catch - the Green fishery which involved the cleaning and salting of fish on board ship but required vast amounts of sea salt or the Dry fishery (sometimes described as Yellow) which required a shore base where the cod could be cleaned and dried. Green or salted cod sold for less than dried cod but the speed of processing allowed the ships to make two fishing trips in one season. The Dry fishery on the other hand was a lengthier procedure but in addition to a higher price meant that the fishermen got an extra income from the extraction of cod liver oil which was a source of fuel for lamps and later as a lubricants for machines.

As the fishing season ended in late August, it meant that the fishermen had to wait until the middle or end of September while the last of the catch was processed before sailing for home. During this time they traded with the local Indians for furs, which in turn created a great demand for North American beaver pelts in Europe.

Island entrepreneurs began to set up trading posts in Newfoundland, Labrador and around the coast of the Gulf of St Lawrence. The Villeneuves were in Placentia before 1655 and Thomas Bandinel was in Harbour Grace in 1675. By 1718 other Jersey firms operating in the Newfoundland area were Carteret Dean, De Carteret & Co, Thomas Denton, Marett and Thomas Seale all of St Aubin.

adventure

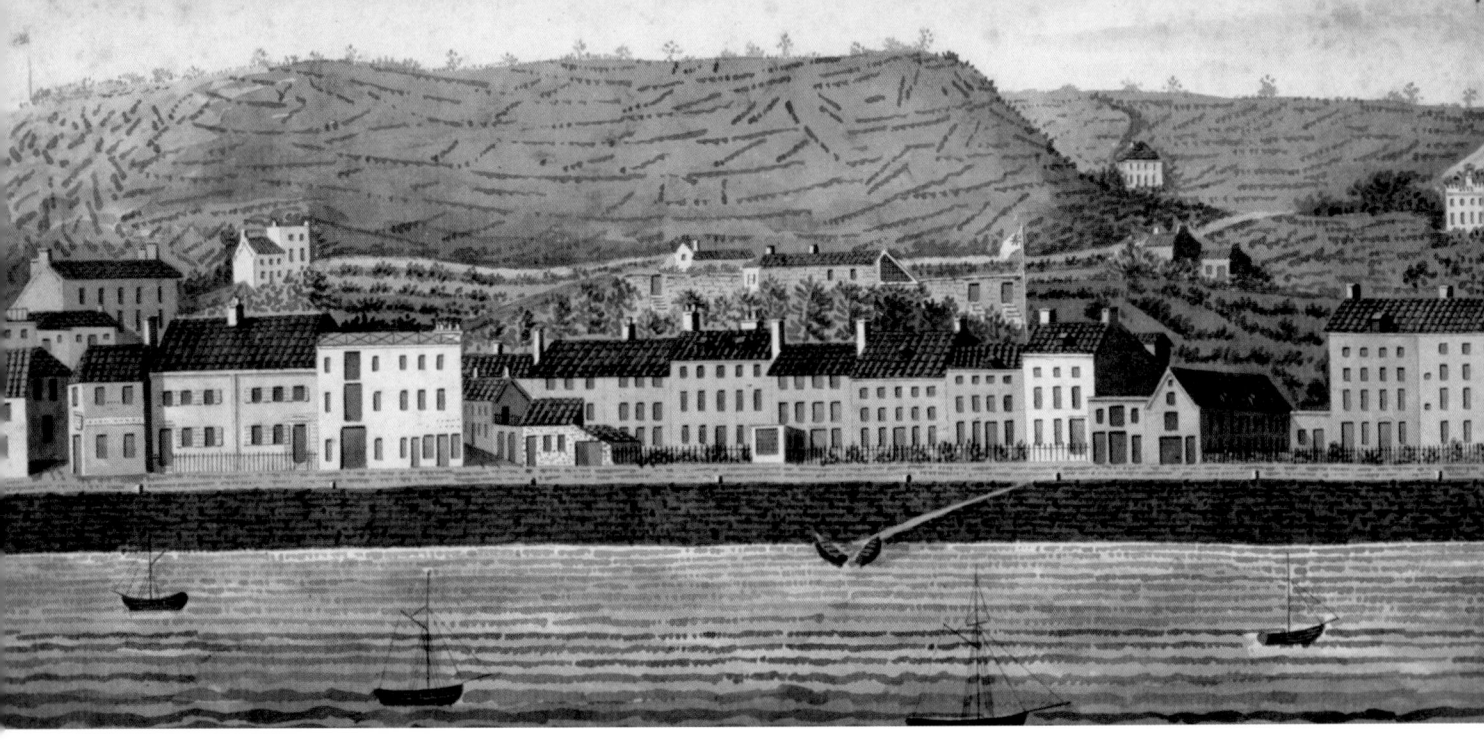

Above
The Bulwarks, St Aubin *c*.1800

Above Right
Map of Gaspe – There are two theories about the origins of the name of "Gaspé" both of which are from the Mi'kmaq language - gespeg meaning "land's end" or gespedeg meaning "last-acquired" as it was the last area the tribe took from the Iroquioian Mohawk tribes.

The political situation in the Americas changed following the British victory in the Seven Years War (1756-63) because by the Treaty of Paris Britain took possession of French Canada and this opened up areas such as the Gaspé peninsula for commercial exploitation by Jersey firms. Although there had been small scale involvement in the late seventeenth century with Henry & John Le Cras and Nicolas Bailhache at Bonaventure in the 1670s, the great change came in 1766 when Charles Robin arrived to trade salt for cod and furs in the Paspébiac which was on the Chaleur Bay side of the Gaspé. Initially Robin was agent for his uncle's firm Robin, Pipon & Co which had recently moved out of Newfoundland to establish themselves at Arichat and Chéticamp in Cape Breton. However, he soon saw the advantages of working for himself. Unlike his competitors, Robin stayed the winter to develop his business and apart from the five years he had to return to Jersey due to the disruption caused by the American Wars of Independence, he remained there until his retirement in 1802 when the business was taken up by his nephews.

The autumn is still to come
And we must weigh our cod.
The Jerseymen with their balances,
Their balances and false weights,
Go from beach to beach,
Collecting what they are owed.

When you take them fish,
They are as gentle as a lamb.
But when you go to their stores,
They are as fierce as lions.
They don't look you in the eye
As they turn their back on you.

In autumn, they return to Jersey,
Making fun of the French.
And in spring, they come back,
Loaded with rotten biscuits,
That they sell pound by pound.

L'automne n'est pas encor venu
Qu'il faut peser la morue.
Les Jersiais, avec leurs balances,
Leurs balances et leurs faux poids,
Ils s'en vont de grave en grave,
Ramasser ce qu'on leur doit.

Quand vous prenez du poisson,
Ils sont doux comme des moutons.
Vous allez à leur boutique,
Ils sont rudes comme des lions,
Ne vous regardent pas en face
Et vous virent les talons.

L'automne, ils vont à Jersais,
En se moquant des Français.
Et, le printemps, ils reviennent,
Chargés de biscuits pourris;
Ils les vendent livre à livre,
C'est pour en faire plus de profit.

This period was the heyday of the fishing trade and it is said that in 1775 between 60 and 70 Jersey vessels manned by 1,500-2,000 Jerseymen were involved. However, the growth of a resident population at the end of the eighteenth century meant that the successful firms would be those who were able to adapt to the supply and carrying trades. This entailed developing an economy in which the resident fishermen bought essential supplies on credit from a company store against their future catch. The "truck" system as it was known already existed in Newfoundland but the Robins developed the system in the Gaspé and were soon followed by smaller companies often set up by former employees.

The resident population often saw these Jersey firms as exploiting their honest labour and resented their presence. This is illustrated by a song from Cape Breton which sums up the popular feeling against the companies in many of the outports.

adventure

However, they also recognised the reality that without companies such as the Robins, Le Boutilliers, de Quettevilles and Nicolles there would be no stores and the market for their fish would be much smaller. While there were occasional attempt by New England and Montreal/Quebec traders to buy the resident fishermen's catch for cash most remained with the Jersey firms because they offered a long term commitment to the area.

These company stores provided a focal point for the settlements that sprung up around them – not only for the provision of necessary supplies but also as centres for disseminating news. The small coastal communities were completed with the building of landing stages, wharves, warehouses, drying grounds or "flakes", churches and in some places even ship building and repair yards. While the largest number of ships were built at Paspébiac, the family names of Mabe, Bechervaise, Annett, Brown, Collas, Touzel and Vibert are also remembered for their contribution to the shipbuilding industry at the eastern end of Chaleur Bay and on the bay of Gaspé.

Above
Belle Anse, Malbay

Above Left
Mon Plaisir, St Brelade. The wealth generated by the "Newfoundland" trade returned to the Island and many fine houses were built on the proceeds and were known as "maisons de Terreneuve" or "Cod Houses".

Shore work, Belle Anse, Malbay *c*.1895

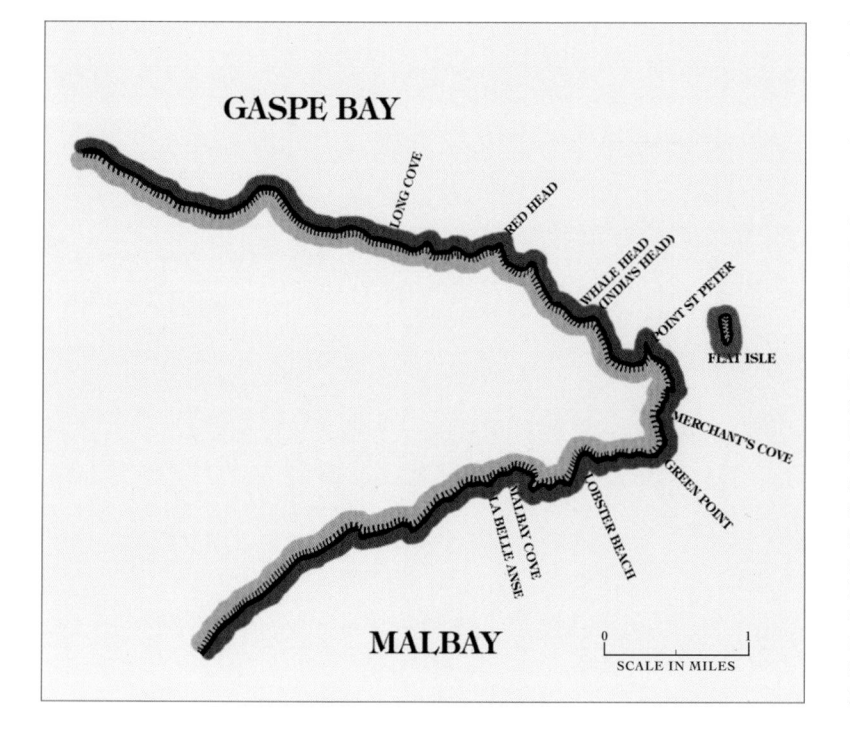

The growing resident population around the Gulf of St Lawrence was made up of French Canadians, American Loyalists, Englishmen from the West Country, Scots and Irish as well as the native Mi'kmaq peoples. Channel Islanders did not settle in great numbers. The Canadian Census showed that in 1851 only 411 people living in Lower Canada (Quebec) had been born in the Channel islands, in 1861 the figure had risen to 628 but had fallen to 482 in 1871 and of these 397 lived on the Gaspé coast – this represented 1.3% of the population of Gaspé at the time. The only significant concentrations of Channel Islanders in Atlantic Canada were in Arichat, Cape Breton, and in Paspébiac in the Gaspé and both of these were headquarters for the large fish companies. Of course these figures did not take into account the children born in the province of Channel Island parents. The only communities in which Channel Islanders represented the majority of the population were Grande-Grave on the Forillon coast and at Malbay/Point St Peter - both in the Gaspé.

settlers

Point St Peter from *Canadian Scenery: District of Gaspé* by Thomas Pye (1866).

In February 1903 the Jersey newspaper, La Nouvelle Chronique printed a description of this engraving. *'The buildings on the left of the view are those of Collas who are gradually extending their business having another establishment at Mal Bay, a third at Gaspé Basin and a fourth on the Shedreck (Sheldrake) River on the north shore of the St Lawrence. The Messrs Collas also have a shipyard. The hull of a vessel on the stocks, their schooner Laurel, may be observed close to the water's edge, to the right of the buildings. They build all the vessels they require for their fish trade, and have now afloat, launched from this spot six vessels, which in point of workmanship and sailing qualities will compare favourably with the generality of Jersey crack vessels'.*

settlers

The few buildings left today give little idea as to how prosperous Point St Peter was 150 years ago when it was one of the most important fishing establishments in the Gaspé. There were over 100 buildings – homes, stores, workshops and warehouses – the quality of which reflected their owners wealth.

A Jersey Settlement

Point St Peter and Malbay – Situated almost halfway between the economic centres of the Gaspé Basin and Percé, Point St Peter is a promontory jutting out into the Gulf of St Lawrence bound by the Bay of Gaspé to the north and Malbay to the south. Its position meant that it was ideally placed to be exploited by fishermen and cod merchants while its hinterland provided land for farming and timber for building. A small cove to the north of the peninsula provided a sheltered anchorage for the settlement's fishing boats and the seashore provided the focus for activity. It was here at the eastern end of the point that a large and important wharf was cut into the rocky outcrop in the late 19th century. This was made strong enough and large enough to cope with the tons of maritime traffic that came into the settlement because in addition to the hundreds of cod boats – both the fishing flats or barges and the carriers, Point St Peter was also the home port to a large number of schooners engaged in the coastal trade and it also received a number of passenger steamers.

During the period of French rule the area seems to have been largely unoccupied – even the Mi'kmaq Indians were thinly spread throughout the region. A small Catholic missionary chapel was built at the end of the 17th century and by the beginning of the 18th century seasonal fishermen were beginning to move into the bay. The first permanent buildings to be set up in Point St Peter were erected by the new breed of merchant traders who were beginning to exploit the fisheries – the Loyalists who began to arrive in the Gaspé around 1776 having been driven away by the rebels at the commencement of hostilities. This group included the Mabe family who built ships at their Corner of the Beach site for several generations.

The Guernsey firm of Carteret Priaulx set up a fishing establishment at Point St Peter at some time during the French Wars (1793-1815) which was then taken over by the Jersey firm of Janvrins as the Guernsey company shifted its activities to the Latin American trade. Eventually Janvrins sold their Point St Peter business to Henry Johnston and their Malbay interests to John Fauvel. Other agencies were set up by Hammond Dumaresq & Co in Malbay and Point St Peter.

The commercial life of the Jersey merchants in Point St Peter, as in the rest of Gaspé, was centred on the catching, curing and the exportation of cod. While smaller merchants such as Alexandre, Le Marquand and Le Gros concentrated their business activities on-shore other Island companies such as the Robins, Nicolles and Fruings saw the opportunities presented by the carrying trade. In Point St Peter this role was filled by John & Elias Collas.

Above
Point St Peter

trade

The firms

A. de Gruchy

House Flag
de Gruchy

John Fauvel – In 1820 the Jersey merchant Abraham De Gruchy bought two lots of land (lots 6 and 7) at Point St Peter and built a house and fishing establishment there. He obviously had men from Jersey do the work as "*C.Powell and Philip J.Carrel of St Peter, Jersey*" is inscribed on a wooden beam in the entrance hall. In 1854 De Gruchy decided to concentrate his efforts in Jersey and sold his interests in Canada. He sold the house and the business at Point St Peter, as well as his shop and land at Malbay to John Fauvel who had previously worked for the Robin Company for over twenty years; first as agent at Percé and then Paspébiac. The house became known as 'Maison Fauvel' and remained in the possession of the Fauvel family until 1936. Within two years of taking over the business Fauvel was employing 6 fishing "barges" and 12 men and he also bought the old Janvrin 'room'[1] in Malbay. When this Malbay 'room' was sold in 1842 it was described as measuring 162 ft at the front and 470 ft deep (1 ¾ acres) and comprising of a dwelling house, stages and fish stores for about 1,000 quintals[2], along with ten Fishing Barges.

Janvrine Cº

House Flag
Janvrin

In 1842 Frederick Janvrin sold up his interests in Gaspé and concentrated on his banking interests instead. It is typical of the Jersey firms' attitudes that the sale should be carried out in St Helier.

J. Fauvel.

House Flag
Fauvel

SALE OF PROPERTY, At Gaspé.

On THE 1st JANUARY, 1842,

WILL BE EXPOSED FOR SALE, IN THE ISLAND OF JERSEY,

IN ONE LOT, THAT

LUCRATIVE ESTABLISHMENT IN THE DISTRICT OF GASPÉ,

LOWER CANADA,

The Property of FREDᴷ JANVRIN, Esq,

COMPRISING

1st.--His principal Establishment, situate at Grand Grève, in Gaspé Bay, four miles from Gaspé Point, including a large DWELLING HOUSE, with suitable FISH STORES to contain about 7000 qtls Fish, Shop, Stages, Cook Rooms, Forge, &c., &c., the whole measuring about 19 chains front by 46 chains long, bounded on the West by Gaspé Bay, and on the East by the River St. Lawrence. *about 150 acres*

2d.--His Property at the Basin of Gaspé, about 15 miles distant from Grand Grève, including a WHARF with sufficient depth of water alongside to admit two Ships of 300 tons, each loading at the same time, with several SALT and FISH STORES, the latter sufficiently spacious to contain 10,000 qtls. Fish. This point of Land is situated on a space of 1 acre, 2 roods, and 22 perches of ground.

3rd.--Malbay, another Establishment, situated to the Southward of Grand Grève, distant 20 miles, with a DWELLING HOUSE, Stages, and Fish Stores, to contain about 1,000 qtls. Fish, where 10 Fishing Barges are kept. This Fishing place measures 162 feet front by 470 feet deep.

4th.--Cape Roziers, another Fishing Establishment, situated in the River St. Lawrence, distant about 2 miles by land from Grand Grève, where 8 Fishing Barges are kept, with DWELLING HOUSE, spacious FISH STORES, &c. The lot measuring about 100 feet front by 180 feet in depth. *about 36 acres*

5th.--Also a beautiful new Establishment, at Griffin's Cove, a well settled spot and sheltered, distant 6 miles from Cape Roziers, with a new Stage thirty-four feet by sixty-four. Also, a new FISH STORE to contain 1000 qtls. Fish, a SALT STORE, Flakes, Cook Rooms, for 10 Barges and Shoresmen. Also, a DWELLING HOUSE,--the whole completed in 1840. Besides Inventory of Goods remaining at the close of the year's navigation at the above Establishments,--with Debts, &c,

For Particulars and Plans, apply to the Proprietor, in Jersey.

JERSEY, 20th APRIL, 1841.

---

[1] Room was a term used to describe a tract of land on the waterfront of a cove or harbour, together with its facilities, from which the fishery is conducted by Channel Islanders.

[2] A quintal was a measure equivalent to about a hundredweight (50kgs).

Exterior of the Alexandre & Le Marquand shop, Point St Peter in winter, Charles Le Marquand is standing outside. It is interesting to note the temporary porch built over the main door and the bell which signalled the daily routine can be clearly seen on the left of the photograph.

Alexander/Le Marquand/Le Gros – By 1849 James Alexandre of St Ouen who had moved to the Gaspé to better himself had established himself as a trader in Point St Peter. His wife Elizabeth Le Maistre was also from Jersey gave birth to a daughter Alice Rosalia in July 1850. In 1857, as the business grew, Alexandre took on a partner, another St Ouennais, John Le Gresley. He was already familiar with the area and the trade as he had twice served on board the Abraham de Gruchy-owned brigantine *Gem* under Captain Francis Le Marquand. This Alexandre/Le Gresley partnership was dissolved in 1867.

It was about this time that a young clerk arrived in Point St Peter from St Ouen – Charles Le Marquand. By the mid-1860s the Jersey economy was under pressure – the oyster fisheries had all but collapsed and the shipbuilding industry was on its last legs. For young men such as Charles, Jersey offered limited prospects and so the opportunity of a job with Alexandre in faraway Gaspé was an attractive one. Charles Le Marquand did well in his new job and eventually married James Alexandre's daughter, Alice Rosalia. When James died in 1878 Alexandre & Co was run by Charles and his mother-in-law, Elizabeth.

James Alexandre's younger daughter, Mary Annie Louisa Alexandre, who died in 1875 had married another Jersey merchant in Point St Peter, John James Le Gros and had two sons, John James jnr and Thomas Alexander and a daughter, Annie May. When Le Gros died in 1881 Charles and Alice Rosalia were appointed guardians of the children. As there was little provision for a formal secondary education in Gaspé, Charles and Alice sent their own two sons Herbert and James and their two nephews to Oxenford House, St Lawrence in Jersey. It was a convenient arrangement as the boys could spend the school holidays at La Hougette in St Mary, a farm owned by Thomas Le Gros, John's brother.

In 1888 Charles decided that it was time for consolidation and expansion and so the business was re-named Alexandre & Le Marquand and in the following year he applied for a trademark to be registered so that he could sell 'dry codfish'.

In 1893 the Le Marquands and Le Gros formed a new partnership and the Jersey circle was completed in 1895 when John James Le Gros married Edith Emily Le Gresley (the daughter of Alexandre's first partner John Le Gresley).

A new and larger store measuring 45 x 28 feet was built about 1898 when the company became known as Le Gros Bros. John James ran the new store at Point St Peter while Thomas opened a branch at Barachois and Charles's eldest son James Le Marquand moved to Belle Anse where he built a new house and shop.

In 1907 Charles Le Marquand died and the business was put into jeopardy when John James began an ambitious scheme to enlarge his house at Point St Peter. The inevitable happened in 1916, the company over-extended itself and became bankrupt with debts of $12,194.30. The assets at Point St Peter and Belle Anse totalled $4,073.73. The Le Gros brothers managed to survive and continued to trade at Barachois until 1923 and at Point St Peter until 1950.

The *Dewdrop* off Corbière, Jersey in 1879 by PJ Ouless

The *Dewdrop* (O.N.69381) was a 101-ton schooner built in Point St Peter, Gaspé in 1875 in the yard owned by the Jersey firm of J & E Collas. Although she was insured in Jersey she was registered in the port of Gaspé in Quebec. This was a device used by a number of the Jersey firms to ensure that their assets were not all in one jurisdiction.

The *Dewdrop* was operated by the Collas' company who acted as agents to carry cod down to markets in Brazil or the West Indies. They then loaded up with a cargo such as coffee, sugar, cotton and timber for England before returning to the Gaspé via Jersey where the Company would send out instructions for their agents, any further cargo and a few apprentices or passengers.

Her end came in 1884 when according to *La Nouvelle Chronique* she left Turks Island on January 16 bound for Jersey but was abandoned on February 3 at 37°N 47°W after she had been dismasted in a storm. Her crew was picked up by the schooner *Sigrlinn* bound for London from Trinidad.

trade

Left

The *Boadicea* was a 106-ton schooner built
in the Collas yard in Point St Peter in 1860
for their own use.

Right

The Collas and Slous store in Gaspé *c.*1900.
Inset The company house flag was four
alternating red and blue horizontal stripe.

J&E Collas & Co – Of the three fishing enterprises described by Thomas Pye during his visit to Point St Peter in 1866 - John & Elias Collas Co., John Fauvel Co and Alexandre et LeGresley – the most important was the John & Elias Collas Co.

The name Collas had been linked to Point St Peter as early as the 1830s when Samuel J Collas was building ships for the Perrées here. Both families came from the parish of St Mary in Jersey and Collas was married to one of John Perrée's daughters. He was also the agent for the Perrée Co and so lived in the community with his family of five children.

The brothers John and Elias Collas both worked for the Robin Company before setting up on their own. They bought the former Janvrin business from Henry Johnston and the Perrées interests in Point St Peter in 1851. In 1856 they had 20 fishing barges and 30 shore workers and in 1866 they had a second establishment in Malbay. They had a large store in Gaspé and expanded on to the north shore of the St Lawrence with a third establishment at Sheldrake. They were one of the bigger Jersey firms in the region and by 1870 they employed 300 fishermen and 300 *greviers* (shore workers who dried the cod). However they were affected by the recession in the trade experienced by the Island firms which followed on from a number of financial scandals in Jersey in the 1870s and 1880s. In 1882 their workforce in Gaspé had shrunk to 50 fishermen and 25 *greviers* although they did still have a number of stores including the one in Point St Peter as well as their fleet of ships with which they carried cargoes of cod to markets in South America, the Mediterranean and Spain.

The brothers set up the head office in St Helier in 1861 and operated from premises in Hope Street until 1879 when they moved to No 2 Commercial Street where they remained until they closed in 1903.

In 1886 following the Jersey Banking Company crash J&E Collas merged with Charles Robin Co and a new company Charles Robin, Collas & Co was created however in Jersey both companies retained their own offices until 1889 when the Robins moved out of their Ordnance Yard premises and shared the Collas office until 1897 when they moved to their own premises in 12 Commercial Street.

As part of the merger deal one of the Collas vessels was altered to provide cabins and a dining area to cater for the annual crossing of the young men who had signed on as apprentices from Jersey to Gaspé (it was the policy of C.R.C to only recruit in Jersey). The vessel chosen was the 155-ton brigantine *Dawn* built in the Collas Yard in Point St Peter in 1874.

Although an optimistic report on the state of the Collas Company in Point St Peter appeared in the Jersey newspaper *La Nouvelle Chronique* in February 1903 the company collapsed the following year when Charles Robin, Collas & Co. moved their headquarters from Jersey to Halifax, Nova Scotia and were subsequently taken over and renamed Robin, Jones and Whitman.

trade

truck **truck**

The Store "...everything from baby powder to coffins,"

These stores were the centre of life in the settlement and sold everything from imported clothes, paraffin lamps and food to snowshoes and fish hooks. They also served as post offices and were centres from which community gossip was disseminated. In a society in which cash was not readily used, a family's subscription to the church and rental of a pew could also be placed on a store account. The company stores were the symbol of the way in which Jersey merchants controlled the economy of the settlements in that they extended credit to the local population but in return ran a monopoly in which they fixed their own prices. Because cash was not generally used in the in the Gaspé in the late eighteenth and nineteenth centuries, the Jersey merchants were very reliant on the credit system. The cash price charged for items was related to the truck or credit prices in that the latter was essentially the cash price with a premium charged to cover the cost of the credit. This premium was usually between 25% and 40% but could reach up to 100%; and this, of course, had the effect of reducing the fishermen wages in real terms.

It was by running the stores that families such as the Le Marquands and Le Gros were able to build their lavish homes and send their children back to Jersey for education.

Above
Inside the Alexandre & Le Marquand shop at Point St Peter.

Left
The Alexandre Le Marquand store at Belle Anse.

praise

*Nouotre péthe,
tch'es dans les cieux...*

The Church

The Anglican Church played an important role in everyday life for Jersey families in the Gaspé. The services were identical to those they had left behind in the Island and this continuity gave the new arrivals a sense of security. A church was built in Point St Peter to serve the growing community but like most of the buildings there it has now disappeared. However, St Peter's Church in Malbay still bears testimony to the devotion of the Jersey settlers; many of the internal carvings were carried out by John Le Cocq, one of Robin's beach-masters. It was not unusual for marble headstones for the dead to be shipped out from Jersey and today the cemetery at St Peter's Church, Malbay bears silent witness to the number of Jerseymen and women who died far from their native shores.

Above
St Peter's church, Malbay taken by James Le Marquand in the opening years of the twentieth century. The departing congregation were attaching their horses to their sledges, known as cutters, for their homeward journey in the deep snow. Many islanders were buried in this churchyard, the tombstone often having been brought out from Jersey.

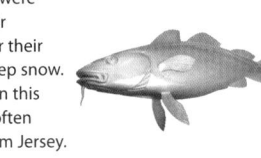

everyman

Thomas David Le Page

Farmers and artisans

Of course not all Jerseymen who went to Gaspé were merchants or fishermen. Some went out as farmers or artisans.

One such was Thomas Le Page who was born in St Mary in 1814. Thomas was 21 when he signed on board the Robin Company snow[3], the *Seaflower*[4]. Life at sea must have suited Thomas because he spent the next six years as a sailor. In 1836 he married Betsey Misson of St Mary and together they had four children before he retired from the sea in 1841 – Betsey Elizabeth born 1836, Nancy born in 1838 and twins, Thomas David and Mary, born in 1841.

Thomas joined his brother-in-law, David Misson of La Tombette, St Mary, in a property deal which went sour and so in 1843 they both moved their families to Gaspé to avoid bankruptcy. Le Page built a house on lot 10 on the Belle Anse Road in Point St Peter and made a successful living for himself and his family as farmer on his 114-acre lot. Thomas and Betsey had another six children in Point St Peter, the last was born in 1857 and, fellow Jerseyman, James Collas was a sponsor. In 1860 Thomas drowned in a fishing accident and his sister Elizabeth went out to Gaspé to help Betsey look after the children. David Misson died in Malbay in 1879 but his widow lived in Belle Anse until her death in January 1908 at the great age of 81.

[3] A two masted vessel similar to a brig.
[4] The mate on the *Seaflower* was Thomas Le Gros, father of John Le Gros the Gaspé merchant who was the father of John James Le Gros.

23

everyman

Two unidentified men posing outside the new store at Point St Peter.

Thomas' eldest son, Thomas David worked as a caulker in the Collas and Co. shipbuilding yard at Point St Peter and in 1879/80 he married 21 year old Susan Jane Coutanche from Jersey. Sadly she died in childbirth in 1883. Four years later Thomas David Le Page went to Jersey and in 1888 he returned with his new wife Mary Ann Le Marquand.

Mary Ann was no stranger to Thomas David or Point St Peter as she had spent her childhood there. Her father Captain Francis Le Marquand as master of the de Gruchy vessel Gem had traded from Point St Peter and when he gave up the sea he took his family out to Canada to start a new life. In 1855 he bought lot 11 on the Belle Anse Road and began work acting as a shipping agent for the Jersey merchants in the area. It was not, however, a good time to emigrate to Gaspé, as by the middle of the 1860s the economy had begun to slow down and the 1871 census in Jersey shows that Mary Ann, her brother Francis Elias and her mother had returned to the Island while her father continued to travel between Jersey, Newfoundland and Gaspé working. The house and land on the Belle Anse Road was sold to fellow Jerseyman James Syvret who had married Thomas David's sister Nancy Le Page in December 1856.

When Mary Ann returned to Point St Peter she took with her the mahogany furniture she had inherited from her mother. Sadly Mary Ann did not enjoy married life for long as she died in April 1889, twelve days after giving birth to a healthy son Francis James on 28 March.

In the early 1840 Thomas John Touzel left the shipyards of Jersey to work in the Perrée shipyards in Point St Peter. In February 1845 his wife Suzanne Elizabeth gave birth to a daughter Esther Elizabeth in Point St. Peter; the following year the first son, Thomas John was born in Malbay; in 1849 the family were back in Point St Peter for the birth of another daughter Jullianna; in September 1851 they were in Barachois for the birth of Caroline Elzada before their last child, another daughter Mary Ann was born in Malbay in 1854.

In 1871 Thomas John Touzel jnr married Mary Ann Le Gresley in St Peter's Church, Malbay.

In any community at this time the blacksmith was an important figure as he made everything from hinges to horseshoes. He made many of the tools needed on the farm and in the shipyard, on the fishing barges and ships. The Collas Company had their own blacksmith shop and through the 1860s Thomas Lempriere was the man in charge.

Left
Jerseymen, Archie Vardon and Clifford Lucas carrying a hand barrow loaded with cod outside the Alexandre & Le Marquand shop at Point St Peter c.1899. Standing to the right of the door is Horace Devouges who was married to Eliza Elvina Syvret – Thomas David Le Page's niece.

carrying

Left
The *Waterwitch* of Jersey built in Point St Peter 1841 entering Palermo. Sicily.

Far Left
An eighteenth century print of the Pereé, Gaspé before the two arches which gave it its name collapsed. *Insert* The *Seaflower* in a storm in the Atlantic, 1839.

The Voyage

Once the catch was cured the merchants chartered one of the carrying firms who usually worked on a commission to take their product to markets. In Point St Peter J & E Collas acted as agents for Alexandre & Le Marquand charging a commission of 1¼% (3d in the £). The main markets for Gaspé cod was South America, the Mediterranean or Spain. All sorts of vessels were used in the carrying trade although brigs and brigantines tended to dominate and the Jersey vessels were usually manned by Jersey masters and crews as the trading voyages usually started and ended in the Island. As well as being capable navigators, the masters of these vessels had to be meticulous in their record keeping which is why so much paperwork surrounding the cod trade has survived.

While the Gaspé cure cod generally had an excellent name, individual companies could easily lose their reputation and the Alexandre Le Marquand Company suffered badly in the mid-1890s. On the 15 January 1895 the brigantine *Red Rose* arrived in Rio de Janeiro from Gaspé with 713 tubs of dried cod marked with the company's distinctive logo but when the English company P.S.Nicolson and Co. inspected them on the 5th February they were shocked by the condition of the fish. Writing to the Collas office in Commercial Street, St Helier Nicolson explained that they were in such a poor condition they had to conduct a survey of the cargo, witnessed by independent observers, and sell everything as quickly as possible. The report of the sale on the 7th February, made by Watson, Ritchie & Co from Lloyd's of London, explains that 36 tubs had been so damaged by sea-water they could not be put up for public auction and were sold for 40 dollars each (40 milreis) in cash while the remaining 535 tubs of *'very poor stuff'* was sold to Luis Augusto de Magalhaes and Bastos for 3 shillings a tub, making £80 5shs. A similar situation occurred in September the same year when 448 tubs unloaded from the Raulin Robin & Co brigantine *85* were found to be *'more or less imperfect in cure. . .sweated and irregular'* and in August 1896 when 362 tubs unloaded from the Fauvel brigantine *Zingara* were found to be *'dark in colour, very mixed and apparently insufficiently cured'*.

It was possibly this loss of reputation that made the company change its name to Le Gros Bros in 1898.

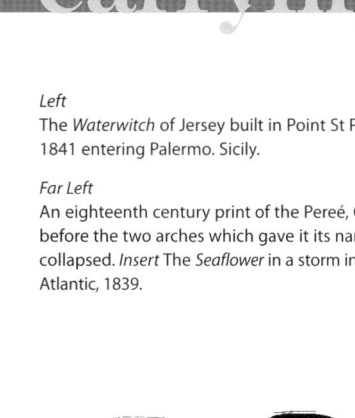

Above
The Alexandre/Le Marquand trademark, 1889. As dried cod would have been loaded into identical wooden tubs it was necessary to stamp each tub with the trade mark, or logo as we would call it today, of the producer.

shipbuilding

Shipbuilding in Point St Peter and Malbay

Following the Napoleonic Wars Jersey developed into being one of the leading shipbuilding centres in the British Isles. Ships were not only built to serve Jersey firms they were also bought by large firms from the mainland because building costs were about £3 per ton cheaper than English yards. However, in the Gaspé the Jersey firms had begun as early as the 1790s to operate shipbuilding and repair yards. The main centre was at Paspébiac where the Robins had their yard but as the number of ships used in the carrying trade increased other Jersey firms set up their own yards. The second most important centre was the eastern end of the Bay of Malbay where there were yards at the Corner of the Beach site owned by several generations of the Mabe family who also built at nearby Cannes de Roches and the Jersey owned yard in Point St Peter operated by the Perrées – Philip, John snr and John jnr – first of all and then the Collas brothers, John and Elias.

The shipwrights in charge of the Jersey operation have been recorded as Samuel Collas (1831-41), Thomas John Touzel and Philip Gaudin.

VESSEL	BUILT	TONNAGE & RIG	SHIPWRIGHT
Adventure	1823	115-ton brig *	Peter Mabe
Amity	1842	brigantine	
Aura	1859	90-ton brigantine	
Boadicea	1860	106-ton schooner *	
Brothers	1858	173-ton brig *	Thomas John Touzel
Chance	1845	123-ton brigantine *	
Chance	1863	134-ton brigantine *	
Charles	1836	59-ton schooner *	John Gerrard Samuel Collas
Charming Nancy	1825	148-ton brig	Peter Mabe, jnr
Concordia	1831	26-ton schooner *	John Gerrard
Conquest	1841	145-ton brigantine *	Peter Mabe
Damon	1831	141- ton brig *	Samuel Collas
Daisy	1890	70-ton schooner	
Dawn	1874	154-ton brigantine *	Philip Gaudin
Dewdrop	1875	101-ton schooner	
Doris	1827	169-ton brig *	Peter Mabe, jnr
Dove	1839	40-ton schooner *	Joseph Roderique
Ellen	1847	55-ton brigantine	
Farmer	1841	133-ton brig *	Samuel Collas
Francis	1828	84-ton brigantine	
Gaspé	1831	77-ton schooner	
Gaspé	1848	97-ton brigantine	Edward Mabe
Guano	1844	172-brigantine	Damase Bouchard
Guess	1836	145-ton brig *	Samuel Collas

* Registered in Jersey

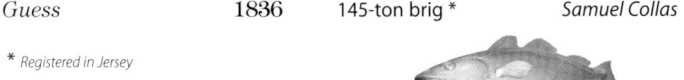

VESSEL	BUILT	TONNAGE & RIG	SHIPWRIGHT
Hasty	1859	46-ton schooner *	
Hazard	1803	schooner	
Hero	1826	310-ton barque	
Highland Jane1	1853	70-ton schooner	
Horatio	1836	71-ton brigantine	*Edward Mabe*
Intrepid	1849	68-ton schooner *	
Laurel	1865	72-schooner	
Marie Victoria	1823	39-ton schooner *	
Mary Queen of Scots	1872	109-ton schooner	
Ocean Queen	1844	123-ton brigantine *	*Thomas John Touzel*
Orleans	1875	209-ton brigantine	*Nap Warren*
Philippa	1840	125-ton brigantine	*Damase Bouchard*
Reward	1853	60-ton schooner *	
Samuel	1838	27-ton schooner *	*Samuel Collas*
Samuel	1865	72-ton schooner	
Speedy	1872	65-ton schooner	
Swallow	1813	28-ton schooner	
Union	1847	99-ton brigantine	*Peter Mabe*
Wag	1815	72-ton brigantine *	
Warrior	1855	100-ton schooner	
Warrior	1864	93-ton schooner	
Water Witch	1841	58-ton schooner *	*Thomas Boyle*
William Pitt	1840	199-ton brig *	*Samuel Collas*

* *Registered in Jersey*

The decline

Life in Point St Peter continued to prosper even after the disastrous bank crash in Jersey in 1886 forced the Robin Company to merge with J & E Collas. The small community even experienced a mini boom with 1894 seeing the establishments at Point St Peter and Mal Bay producing a record quantity of 5,000-5,500 quintals. However, the Jersey firms were finding it harder and harder to make ends meet and so gradually the fishery was wound down. The introduction of a regular steamship service reduced the number of small coasters using the harbour.

In 1912 the railway finally arrived in Gaspé Basin, which meant that the region was no longer dependent upon the coastal shipping link with Montreal and Quebec. When the Canadian government finally extended its road network right around the Gaspé peninsula in the 1920s and early 30s the area benefited from tourism. The Fauvel House was even turned into a hotel in 1933 – Shirley Temple stayed there in 1942 – but by 1948 even tourism began to fail. Apart from lumbering there was little to keep the young in the community and instead of bringing prosperity and development to the isolated communities, the much heralded road became the way out and so the younger generation found work in Montreal and Quebec leaving the older people behind. As the communities died out or were deserted, the family homes were only used for holidays or, in some cases, burned to avoid having to pay taxes.

Chasing the Cod

JERSEYMEN IN CANADA

First published Jersey 2007
By the Jersey Heritage Trust
Jersey Museum, The Weighbridge, St Helier,
Jersey, JE2 3NF

ISBN 978-0-9552508-3-5

Acknowledgements
The author would like to thank the
following people for their help, advice and
contribution of material for this work:
Jeannot Bourdages, Barbara Carmé, Jane
Edwards, Marian Kirkbride, and all his
colleagues from the Jersey Heritage Trust
who supported him during its writing.

Images supplied by

Jersey Heritage Trust / Société Jersiaise Collection 7, 8, 14, 16, 18, 26 & 27

Marian Kirkbride 23

MLP Trust 27

Musée de la Gaspésie - Centre d'archives de la Gaspésie Front, 5, 11, 13, 15, 20, 21, 22, 22, 24, 25 & 25

Société Jersiaise Photographic Archive 3, 6, 10, 10 & 19

Note
The spelling of names is always problematical during this period as Islanders wrote in both English
and French, therefore, for consistency throughout the publication where names differ they have
been set down in their English/Jersey form.
Placenames: Point St Peter and Malbay instead of Pointe St-Pierre and Malbaie.
Christian names: Francis, James, John instead of François, Jacques, Jean.
Surnames: Alexandre, Le Gros and Le Gresley instead of Alexander, LeGros and LeGresley.

Further reading
Alexander, D & Ommer, R (ed) (1979): *Volumes not Values*
Fischer, L.R. & Sager, E.W. (ed) (1979): *The Enterprising Canadians*
Jameson, A. (ed) (1986): *A People of the Sea*
Jean, J (1982); *Jersey Sailing Ships*
Marcil, E.R. (2000): *On chantait <<Charley-Man>>*
McDougall, D.J. *"Gaspé built square-rigged sailing ships"*. Gaspésie, vol. XXIX, no. 3-4 (115-116),
septembre-décembre 1991: p. 69-82
Ommer, R. (1991): *From Outpost to Outport*
Ommer, R. (ed) (1990): *Merchant Credit & Labour Strategies*